Passing For Normal
Poems and Stories

by Lucia Blinn

Passing for Normal
Poems and Stories by Lucia Blinn

Published by First Flight Books
A division of Bruce Bendinger Creative Communications, Inc.
2144 N. Hudson • Chicago, IL 60614
773-871-1179 • FX 773-281-4643
www.firstflightbooks.com • www.Luciablinn.com

FIRST FLIGHT BOOKS

1 3 5 7 9 10 8 6 4 2

Book Design: Meredith Raub
Cover Photograph: Steve Ewert
Cover Design: Alvin Blick

For further information, you may e-mail the author:
lrblinn@aol.com or visit her website: www.Luciablinn.com

For Meredith, Daphne and Scott
and for Jim

The Poems

The Stories

The Poems

Charlotte's Web Site

Don't you believe it.
Surely, E.B. White or Andy,
as I too might have called him,
had I lived back then, and why didn't I?
would have resisted the teching
of his enchanting spider even as I
wince at commercials that
can't end without dot coms and hold
fast to ground that crumbles
beneath aging Ferragamos.
Yes, and I'd have passed on Mr. Ford's
remorselessly horseless carriage.
True, we perished for want of penicillin,
but surely we might have stopped there.
Must Sputnik have spun an end
to life as we knew it that
Madison Avenue morning parading
as any other?

Where is my pale hair trailing ribbons?
Where is my drift of white gown?
Where is Mr. Darcy?

Passing For Normal

Do not be deceived. True, my skin
appears whole. No tape or ooze,
no threatening seam reveals
that I am not, as they say, all together.

My clothes are no clue: they bear the
requisite labels du jour. The skeleton in my
closet causes fabric to drape in agreeable
shape and you are ha! further deluded.
My home? You are not getting warmer.
A welcoming hug of comfort and color,
familial, functional, heirloomed. Ah,
you say, just what I'd expect. Yet available
to all who majored in Barbara Darcy's Rooms
at the University of Bloomingdales
in the sixties, minored in House & Garden,
prayed to Sister Parish, and had an
antiques-collecting mother-in-law.

My chatter is a good cover.
An early shyness diminished with practice,
I converse on the odd book and film,
restaurant and movement of the moment.
Smart and Clever, Exciting and Fun,
ran the testimonials of two former beaux
of admittedly brief duration. So far,
so normal. Yet just beneath the style
that dangles a gold bangle and gets the joke
on the beat skitters a jingly-jangly
fourteen-year-old sham
who knows nothing for sure.

Passing For Normal

I look, no stare, at convincing adults
and marvel. How is it they choose?
Decide? Add? Divide?
Stop at one of anything?
These garden-variety breathers put keys
to locks and doors open the first time.
In their cars, they unfold origami that
gets them there. They pass the bar;
they do not go in.

It is a case of misgiven identity.
I was to be blonde and beautiful,
but they gave that to Beverly White
so she got to be homecoming queen
and dance with Flanagan, and I got
the silver sack of words.

Give Up This Day

Eleanor Roosevelt said:
"You must do the things you think
you cannot do." I am not sure she meant
live without Tareytons and martinis,
the garden variety we sloshed in the sixties,
and serial Starbucks and Diet Coke on the phone,
in the tub, and everywhere in between. But it
has come to that because everything I like,
I like in multiples. A legendary advertising drunk said:
"Make 'em doubles and keep 'em coming."
Sign me up. Cappuccinos. Cognacs.
Men. Millions. Who was it who said: One is none?
I said that.

These Spartan days, none is the wiser.
Thank you for not smoking.
It was the elegant Kents that killed elegant Irma.
Thank you for not wining while dining.
Just one sip makes me horribly stiff.
Thank you for kissing off Diet Coke.
My semi-dearly, but totally departed,
know-it-all spouse said: You need that sauce
intravenously.
Aspartame?
There are rumors of tumors.

But, what if Woody Allen nailed it in Sleeper
and, years from now, the bad stuff
is the good stuff and we are fed
dire warnings of the repercussions
of failing to ingest our minimum
daily requirement of crême brulée?
Well, what if?

This Is Not Working

You think this is easy? This daily reinventing
that I might catch the driverless
coach and find a seat? The cosmic joke,
another in a humorless series, is that working is
work and not is bliss. A lie of the patent variety.
Remember the New Yorker cartoon?
Failure: the bum on a desert isle.
Success: the man behind a desk.
Failure failed to show the effort
in not showing up. Success is a snap:
get up, get dressed, get going,
do what they say, take home the pay.

Blair said the hardest part was waking up
and hearing the fire bell only there was no fire.
Only there is, Blair, and we are not invited.

Which is the problem. Much as I craved the
blaze that year after motherhood
is how it is now. My rooms are not my rooms
between eight and six. Dust bunnies
yearn for privacy. The machine itches to answer.
The refrigerator groans: can't I chill in peace? Let them.
Give me the moans and nervous laughter of
downtown souls who pirouette their papers
in that anxious ballet.

You didn't retire, you cashed in, they said. So, yes,
right on schedule, I am taking the long walks and
reading the long books that, until the minute I got to them,
sounded like the goal of holies.

So this is how it is to be a senior before the junior is cold.
This is the shrieking beneath the nursing home rocking.
Wait a minute. I wasn't finished.

Out Of The Loop

Where shall I put this? I asked the hostess,
indicating the remaining Tetrazzini.
In that Baggie, she said. All right. Is everybody
in this country stuffing goopy leftovers into
floppy bags while I store mine
in stiff-upper-lid Tupper sort of ware?
Stick celery sticks in a bag
or part of a pomegranate.
But an unmade bed of noodles
in a puddle of cream sauce?
Why is that a good idea? Judy says
it's because I have a normal-size fridge
and don't understand that Baggies
take less space. Does everyone live
with Barbiesque appliances?
No, there is a more sinister explanation.
Did I get the memo saying it was time
to let my watch dangle?
That having it fit snuggly was passé?
Never mind you can't read its face
face down. File that under boring detail.

And how is it mine are the only sweat pants
that still cover my ankles? When
did shrinking the be-jeesus out of them so they
come to mid-calf come to be? Or do
you buy them that length?
What do you ask for? Really stupid sweats
of the pedal pusher variety?

I won't start on wearing the hideous back
of a baseball cap in front while the brim
that once kept the sun off your face and the
squint from your eyes is shading your neck.
Or why it's cool to drive a truck.
Or cool to say cool.

Someone has deleted my name
from the mailing list of what's hot.
Bless you.

Half Time

Assuming our souls are recycled,
I was once an empress;
you, a serial killer or John the Baptist.
The milk of amnesia, however, means
I have no memory of my empire.
Do you remember your sentence?
Or severance?

Rather than dying to start over,
we might, at mid-life, switch sides.
Trade, say, bank accounts.
Have haves become have-nots.
A pauper would peer in a mirror
and see an heiress.
An heiress would do windows in Paris.
Welfare moms would wear Armani.
Armani, Salvation Army.

No, no, you protest.
I worked hard for this LexusDuplexRolex.
So, actually, did I.
The sticky wicket being,
to the homeless, I am a have-and-a-half;
to Mr. Micro, barely a byte.
Comparisons are odious.
This game, dangerous.
Feasting is more fun than fasting.
Doing with more, more marvelous
than without. (I think.)
Nothing to do but play this hand
and wait for the next.
Do excuse me, though, I'm late for a fitting.
If it isn't one ball gown, it's another.

Hell's Bells

A cellphone rang on Yom Kippur—
in the synagogue.
Then one went off in the loo.
Yesterday, the ghost of Ed Norton emerged
from a manhole chatting, presumably,
to the bus driver. "...zat you, Ralphie?"

Do you like being rung bidding no trump?
In the midst of a row?
Exchanging your vows?
Once there was a commodity
called privacy. You could change lanes
without commentary. Squeeze a cantaloupe
without company. Today, you may not
see a movie or wheel in for surgery—
who is it now? calling to say what?
other than they've got your number.
A pox on these instruments
that give us no quarter.
In quieter days, a cell meant jail.
Hello?

Whatever Happened To One?

Once upon a time, people had one job
from their twenties to their sixties, over and out.
Women kept one man, men one woman,
for better or worse till death.

One simple raincoat, one wristwatch,
one lone dog seemed enough. The family
took but one vacation
and stocked one ice cream at a time.
One TV was more than plenty and even
Jones had only one phone.
A single shoe box held all my treasures,
a rosary all my prayers.

Prosperity banged in with bags and
baggage and one was suddenly none.
Houses and spouses, lipsticks and
lunch dates, cards charging chaos.
Business boomed at the building of Babel.

From one spattered cookbook to whole
new cuisines and now nobody cooks.
Too busy with too many papers
that cover the same bleeding wreck.
Yesterday's Chevy spawned X's and Z's
and all of them drive us crazy.

I am homesick for the solitary, its clarity
and power. One didn't rush and took its sweet
time and saved room for dreaming and humming
and skipping and robins.

The nineties career toward a cluttery end.
And, like the first peep of spring's early shoot,
a singular notion occurs.

Keeper

It is Passover morning and someone outside my window,
six floors down, is whistling the middle part of a hymn.

Twenty years of engineers in this building have included
the improbably tall Mr. Larson who nailed the magnifying mirror
at a perfect height were he the one applying eye shadow.
Joe T., the crabby Croat, whose likeness is in Webster's
under male chauvinist. The man of the house had only
to think Joe to set his esoteric wrenches awhirl.
I had to compose numerous notes
and resort to Blanche DuBois (...fancy my breathing
without your help, Joe. Could you possibly come up
and fix the sink?) before his hulking testosterone appeared.
Then Tom Somebody. He, freshly divorced;
I, newly widowed. (There isn't anything
I wouldn't do for you). Yes, but no.
Did get me in my boudoir though.
Had to install the Levolors, didn't he?
It was Body Heat, hold the bodies.
Yes, but no.

Now Patrick. Know how you can see
the six-year-old in some men's faces? You can
still see Patrick sitting in the first row so Sister
can keep her eye on him, head over his paper,
one eye cruising for trouble. Patrick wears a
gold ring in his ear and sends email
and asks if everything is all right up there
and once said, how you doing, Sunshine?
Patrick smiles at a small brown ball he swears
will not scare me when it turns Rottweiler
and rolls white paint on the driveway
and whistles the Ave Maria.
The boy is a poem.

Losing It

Someone poked through her closet this morning
and pulled out a Nancy Heller linen shirt
that would still be in mine had I not listened to
the thinks-she-knows-all Daphne who channels
Diana Vreeland and said, forget it, Mom,
in that way that defies me to disagree.
It was the blue of a Caribbean sky
played against a sexy tan.
Too neon for a mother of a certain age?
But why do I miss it in Mexico,
that blue the very hue for margaritaville?

If only I had a basement like Julie's grandmother
who has in hers her every evening bag.
Mrs. Robinson, the original,
trots out one vintage stunner after another
while I mourn a long-gone inky Gucci,
a Joan Crawford moiré envelope from Neiman's,
when you went to Dallas to go to Neiman's,
and a navy faille heart from seventh grade.
Gone too are black leather jeans from Peaches in Aspen.
They had shrunk, somehow, but so, somehow, have I.
And Bertie's pound of deco diamonds bracelet
I thought not me. I sold it only to see
a facsimile in Town & Country
looking like nothing so much as me.

Updike is inconsolable over the loss of a
boyhood bank. I'll see your piggy, John,
and raise you a pair of rugs.
Thought I didn't need them. Do.
Less, Mr. van der Rohe, is less.

Pregnant

Not a nice enough word for such a lovely time.
Yet With Child is too Virgin Mary,
Enceinte too fussy and French,
Preggers too hopelessly hip.
How to describe this other-body experience?
Mine, so long ago yet so glowy fresh.
An instant flash of golden sweet harmony.
A visit to another realm.
A smiling tête-à-tête
of caring and sharing
and cozy as it gets.

Some women moan at growing round
and wish it over. Don't you.
Enjoy this play;
there is none like it.
It's you and you as never before.
Oh, and him, I suppose;
he does get some billing.
Though you get the delicious dreaming
and resting and sighing
and miracle-making and expectantly waiting
for the gift of a lifetime
you don't get to keep
and might make you weep.
Did anyone tell you?
About free membership
in the Worry Your Pretty Head Off Club?

Johnny Walker

Or maybe it's Jimmy or Jake or Sol
but surely Walker, the slim soul who strolls
by every Saturday, every Sunday, rain or sun,
sleet or snow, in jeans and navy poplin,
sometimes chatting to a partner, but smiling,
always smiling.
What so delights this Howdy Doody,
the top of his sweet head a gleaming circle
ringed with white?
I mean to don sneakers one day,
step in his shadow and glean
his secrets. Then that would be me
lean of limb, loping, nodding,
happy.

Missing

"Here you go, Ma'am."
Did you hear that?
That valet called me Ma'am.
It wasn't the first time.
We lived on Melrose then,
I, a pioneer supermom,
twitching in an ill-fitting marriage,
crazed enough without a delivery boy
delivering Ma'am. The word,
not a synonym for soigné,
struck my ear like a spark
and singed my very sanctum.

Did he mean me?
Never mind, next time, whoever will say,
"Here you are, Miss," just like always.
Who was I kidding?
Next time, it was, "Thank you, Ma'am."
And next time.
And next time.
Then it was time to know:
No one ever again will see
that Ma'am is not who I am.

The knee that speaks to me?
An aberration.
The silver strands? A fashion statement.
The fact that I need a nap? So did JFK.
So listen up, you grocery clerk,
beneath this Ma'am you think you see,
I am seventeen and John Donahue just called.
Ma'am. Don't give me that.
I am forever a miss.
Well, that too.

Opera Star

Skinny Hetty, under a frozen midnight helmet,
sits in the highest reaches in vocal clothes:
complicated, hairy sweaters in jade, crimson, violet,
burdened with braid and pearls.
A teetering memorial to six-inch heels
whose singular pink echoes a sliver of skirt.
Whole wands of mascara gave their lives here:
inky commas against a lunar face.
Defying gravity, she doesn't sag
from jazzy stones jailed in heavy metal.
I, dressed as silent night, imagine
concocting this aurora borealis,
size four. Imagine matching pinks.

The curtain rises. Hetty is motionless,
enraptured, soul-to-soul with the diva.
At intermission, she conducts getting
coffee with an intensity that parts the sea
of minglers, yet no one minds. Hetty's cells
ignite your own.

When the not-all-that-fat-anymore lady
has sung, Hetty lifts small pale hands high
above her head. Her eyes are shining, wet.

Do you think she bowls two-fifty? Reads Maeve Binchy?
Checks out your peaches at the Jewel?
Cares for an ailing son? Dotes on an
octagenarian who loves her beyond reason?
Find out, will you?

I Miss His Plaids

Understand he was a fetishist.
His shirts, clones of clones,
were chosen with the care
of a neurosurgeon pondering a scalpel.
Not for him anything loud
or, God forbid, logo'd.
Taupe crossed with navy.
Celery with claret.
Hunter green countered with cream.
A particular red—there was a
cheery side; but not Chinese!
not tomato!—squared with teal.
Cotton for summer,
Viyella for fall and winter.
He wore them over undershirts,
crew or invisibly v'd, and under
cashmeres from the Burlington Arcade,
Marshall Field, Land's End (Look at this quality,
will you? And only a hundred-and-fifty).

He bled tendrils of Ivy League.
Not for this Brooks Brother pants
with pleats without cuffs, jackets that slouched,
coats that tied. The merciful One took him
before collars, for all their battened hatches,
fell prey to lewd bands. Ridiculous,
would have been his kindest review.

I miss his tweeds. Disciplined rows
of sotto voce greys and
browns with silent flecks of forest
or burgundy. Trousered variations
on a theme of understatement.
Triple-decked multiples of pet rep ties:
sober maroons, steady navies,
stately golds rolled, after wearing, inside out.
(They iron themselves that way.)

I Miss His Plaids

Giddy mistakes or those that fell from favor
were handed to the brother-in-law
who never had to own his own.

Of course, I miss the jokes.
Not just Abe and Sam and Becky
in that hilarious accent. But the wicked takes
on the passing parade of people
he found wanting. And they were legion.

The clank of keys on the antique plate?
The three-note whistle? I wouldn't mind
hearing those. Or the glad-I-called him,
Hi Kid of an afternoon. There was safety in
that. Or so it seemed.

Lookin' good, he'd allow with authority,
appraising me in the underwear competition,
decades of judging under his belt.
Elegant broad, he'd award when we
were party-bound. A postmortem tabby
keeps his own counsel.

Vintage Paul Newman with brown eyes, he loved
me, warts and all. Anyone who thinks
her ideas world class and abhors compromise
cannot claim immunity to imperfection.
Do I miss the quashing of those ideas
because they invariably involved spending, and he was
spooked by the specter of Not Enough For Retirement?
No. It is the no nay saying, tra la, that has birthed the
buoyant new me.

The Prince Of Pop Art
And Other Claims To Fame

My cousin Laura's husband's nephew, Andrew?
Andy Warhol.
We were near-relations without a ship.
Oh, Andy, how could you die before we had lunch?
Before you left my wall a Warhol?

However. I danced with a man
who danced with a woman
who danced with Fred Astaire.
The man I danced with
was dancing with someone else
except when he sang every lyric
to every love song that Pump Room night.
Thought for a while, was absolutely sure, for a while,
he, Albert Brooks wannabe, was The One.
How we do go on on crumbs
even Gretel couldn't follow.

The big-time tenor? In a navy tent of a robe
in his undressing room?
Playing the Italian card, I give my name
Di Lammermoor fashion.
He holds my cool hand in his moist, beefy one,
then, on my program, draws an elongated fusilli
that reads: Luciano Pavarotti.

Jesse Jackson gave me the eye at Midway.
Warren Beatty in Burbank did not.
Jane Powell at Hudson's said hello fifty years ago.
My brother said, She Did Not.
Then, Oprah. Last year? At the health club?
Looked at me not looking at her until it was too late.
What do you want at six a.m.?
Oprah. Do you suppose she stands in her closet,
her closets, and knows what to put on?
Know what I think?
Like me, like you, she hasn't a clue.

Irma

She was my own Hepburn, chic as Audrey,
spirited as Kate, and some of her bones
were pure Garbo.
Darling! You look ravishing! she sang
at the door of the duplex,
turtlenecked in camel cashmere, skirt skimming
narrow knees, Cartier hoops
swinging with diamonds. Ravishing I am not,
yet Irma's proclaiming made it fact.

In the Wedgwood blue room with Lautrec
sketch, lemon slipper chairs, and jug of orange lilies,
we agonized over men and children
and lamented the miles between us.
(Why do all the best people leave New York?)
At midtown bistros where her hats turned heads,
she heard tales of an empty marriage
and I feasted on the Paris years—dressing
at Balenciaga, entertaining Buchwald,
riding at dawn with Aly Khan.

Her first love reappeared one rainy day,
and they lived blissfully, as she would say,
almost ever after.
He rubbed her shoulders and read her to sleep.
There were quiet nights in her city digs and
dinner parties at his in the country.
Guests were dusty old money who wore musty silk,
forty-year old shoes and hang the look.

Irma

Pick what you want me to leave you,
she said in the duplex at twilight.
Lung cancer.
Not that she ever uttered the words.
And not that he was there, having left her
for Alzheimer.

Get me out of here, she mouthed in the
cruel room at Lenox Hill.

Her two small still-lifes hang on my bittersweet
wall and twenty years of pale blue letters to
Lucia darling or Dearest Lucia are tied in a drawer.

Irma, darling. Dearest Irma.

Overzellous And
For No Good Reason

Why do I wonder what Sam,
Forbes Four Hundred Zellionaire,
is having for lunch?
Because my daughter went to school with
his chef's brother?
Because I have a photo of his wife
from another life?
Because our ancestors may have hoed
adjoining rows in the old country?
Or do I conjure Sam's platinum spoon stirring coffee
from beans from his own mountain
because I have studied the glossy pages long
and well and would wear two billion of wherewithal
as seamlessly, oh, I assure you, as the next Cinderzella.
You would applaud my ability
to choose the quietest jewels
(nothing vulgari from Bulgari),
my discretion at slipping off to Zurich
for the odd shot of whatever they're shooting
insteada placenta these days,
and getting the hang, as did the dead Duchess,
of daily manicures and satin sheets
ironed by hand and left unfolded
lest a crease leave a crease on
my silken thigh.

Ah, to crack crab with Sam Zell.
To have a stab at his filet of filet.
To lay my head on his eight thousand-
dollar pillow and dream the dreams of one
who knows where her next sapphire is coming from.

Just Say Nancy.
Everyone Else Does.

Even as I aver that every other male
is named Bruce or Brian—you think not?
Check menus for chefs.
Scan shirts of fellows who fix things.
Read the cast of B movies
(they aren't called that for nothing).
See Sunday's Safire.
Call my brother-in-law.
Ask Meredith her last three
beaux. Ask my last or, no,
let the sleeping dog lie, he's so good at it.
His brothers and partners?
Bruce and Brian. Bruce and Bryan.
Enough to send one on a Bruce Bendinger.
But I digress from a threat of another gender.
Her name is Nancy and she is legion.

Airline agents do not say
N as in Nevermind, they say Nancy.
As in the woman in red who said say no.
As in a niece who cut me off at the knees.
As in Bernstein & Block. Goodman & Roth.
Cohen & Crane & Drew.
Kissinger's who towers. Herb's who paints.
The Nance in France. Bruce's beauty.
(Can a Brian be far behind?)
The little Fox on Blackmoor.
The model, Dolen, from another poem.
Dennis's, a mere Nan, but landed her man.
La Jordan, who wore us out wearing rarely
the same thing thrice, come Heller high water.
Sinatra sang of a laughing face
to his Nancys, senior and junior.

Just Say Nancy.
Everyone Else Does.

And what of my chum, the Gardner,
and the Farm & Gardener?
One's good green name
and the other's pursuit all but
absolve them from my nattering.

Unconvinced?
Consider Morrison's year-end missive
with mention of mentors:
Nancy B., Nancy G., Nancy L., Nancy, P.;
L., the gone but not forgotten spouse
of my sweetheart whose moniker lives on
in a granddaughterer.

Once, we were plagued with a plethora of
Debora/Linda/Susan. Today, one yearns
for breakfast without Tiffany/Brittany/Ashley.
Yet it is Nancy, you see, the quick and the quiet,
the able and stable, astride her own two syllables,
who appears not to disappear.

Not fancy, yet not without nuance.
Not chancy, not her pursuance.
She is not simply, but ever so surely,
inescapably, inexorably,
Nancy.

Tall Order

I'll have an egg roll, a hot fried egg roll,
hold the cold rubber spring rolls,
and won ton soup and fried rice
from the long-gone Wing Yee.
The chicken salad and coffee shake
Daphne and I devoured in the Drake Drugstore.
A rare cheeseburger, who knew it was dead cow?
from the fallen Acorn on Oak.
Mom's potato soup with sour cream.
Bertie's chicken liver on thin rye with crystal glasses
of scotch in the Long Beach sunroom.
Egg salad on skinny toast at the Brevoort
before soggy sessions with Dr. Lane.
The manicotti the day we bought Meredith
a hand-smocked dress at Teeny Weeny in the Village.
The crock of paté Allan's friends on Park served
when I might have remembered I was married.
The English muffin at Soupburg with the model,
Nancy, who taught me to eat less and makeup more.
A Whamburger from Phoebe's that went up in flames
at two a.m. below my room on Madison.
Carbonnade Flamande James Beard's assistant
I was fixated on fixed in his creamy flat on Bleecker.
My first arugula at Orsini's with the vamp
who sang an arms-flailing Witchcraft
when we were babies at BBDO.
The lobsters in Maine before I knew
I shouldn't marry Marty.
The steak in London before I tried on leaving him.
Zabaglione at Mercurio when I wondered
why I was there with him.

Tall Order

The Chianti salad with the producer
who hoped I wasn't sleeping with the director.
The brandy at the Ritz with the director
I was sleeping with. Slept with. Twice.
The wine at Gunne's party when the divine
and drunken David said he'd love me forever.
The sunny strawberries we picked in the country.
Apple kringle in the country.
Every good thing we ate on the screened porch
in the country, never mind that Marty was dying,
the girls were leaving, and I would be selling.
Oh and waiter? Please hurry.
I'm starving.

The Most Beautiful Girl
In The World

he called his Zosia until the soft May day
her frail ghost sighed its last.
A beauty with slate eyes that spared her
nothing, a once-slender body
that bore a domino of tragedies.
The silent girl from Poland was too shy
to leave her village and study
yet sturdy enough to cross an ocean,
marry and carry too many burdens.
Too few funds. Too little laughter.
Drink and madness in the night.

I picked red tulips that morning before
Perry (Como) put small poodle paws on the
once-forbidden bed before he walked into traffic.

She, who rarely cut more than the odd rose,
tended a casually ordered plot where
no plant sprawled, no weeds snarled.
Yellow hybrids sunned with white daisies,
clumps of yarrow and feverfew that outlive her;
calendula, the color of creamsicles; purple iris, or flags,
she called them, and never enough peonies. Beyond
the sourful cherry tree with limbs for making plans in,
an ancient, fragrant, faintly pink rose climbed the
rickety wire fence between us and the Gillands.
Halloween-painted tiger lilies did their famous backbends.
Hollyhocks hugged the garage like wallflowers.
Elves and fairies danced on moss amid lily-of-the-valley
that rang years ago on my illicit-candlelit altar where
I sang to a blue-robed virgin in the sky.

continued

The Most Beautiful Girl
In The World

Clothes-pinned to apron and housedress,
the world's most beautiful moved among us
like impoverished nobility; elegant and given to edict:
No jeans; they'll make you rough.
No summer camp; there are snakes.
No ballet; do you want big calves?
No playing under the sprinkler on shady days;
polio. No ice water, Coke or Shredded Wheat.
They freeze and rot and scratch your stomach.
No big bows, varsity jackets, Hell!, Damn!,
smoking or sassing. I locked her out one hot afternoon
to scare myself with the well-banked flames of her fury.
Not that she lifted a hand. Not that that
would not have terrified less.

She never stopped cooking, she who hated cooking.
(What should I make for that crazy supper?)
Oatmeal every morning, eggs with floured bacon.
Cabbage soup and mushroom. E-Z cut ham,
a member of the family. Fat shiny roast pork.
Daddy's kielbasa, alchemy in the basement;
a near-explosion once, à la Mr. DePinna.
Friday, clean house day, we celebrated with chocolate
chip cookies made with Crisco which made them moist.
Or cake, the frosting all I ate. And still do. I hungered
for more than set-the-table-peel-potatoes. Can't I cook?
But she couldn't slow down to teach.
Not till two grandsons:
You want to learn? Watch.

The Most Beautiful Girl
In The World

Dressing up meant navy only; black took her back
to the old country. And though she, with her symbiotic
sibling, our beloved merry Ciocia, sewed from scratch
all my things and Tina's—twirly skirts, Chesterfield coats,
Eisenhower jackets Ike may have liked but I despised,
she'd rather restyle; adding lace here,
cutting a collar there.

One cozy Christmas Eve, we were led to see
beneath the tree our everyday dolls newly
gorgeous in gowns of creamy silk and satin
standing shyly, awaiting their wedding.
No small surprise sewn while we were at school
by the woman with no time for frivolity.

On the dreamy day she lay dying, I sat on the stoop
remembering young summers of prescient glimpses
through the lilac and greeny velvet cemetery.
(It's just like a park, she soothed anyone uneasy.)
I would leave that small house with large woes,
none of those for me, and live in a grand place
beside a wide blue sea whitened with gliding sails.
Don't they make you smile, Mom, my boats?

Ich Bin Ein New Yorker

I had it in my hand.
I lived in New York.
I was a New Yorker who browsed
at Bergdorf, lunched at Tiffany,
collected Gucci before copies,
bought Erno Laszlo from Erno Laszlo,
swooned over soufflé at Cafe Nicholson.
New York is a terrible place to visit,
cramming it all in in a few days.
Far better to live here and savor it
slowly.

Choosing the wrong husband is not a good idea.
Not heeding his dreams of leaving New York
can be life-threatening.
He yanked me out of the leafy east side
and plopped me from whence I'd escaped:
the banal pasture, the mid, as in neither
here nor there, west.

They've torn down BBDO on 44th street.
But what was Mrs. Ferguson's Residence
on 68th still stands and I can still see the window
when I was twenty and Françoise Sagan
had just written a book and surely I could too.

Once when I fell and broke my heart,
I flew to the granite arms of Manhattan
for mothering. I booked a table at
Veau D'Or and communed with Irma's ghost.
I made phone calls at the Peninsula
where a tall blonde in black
flashed diamonds and spoke German.
I walked a thousand blocks and
studied a thousand flowers
at Takashimaya. I stepped out of the
speeding path of a redhead in green
tearing for a taxi. And hobbled into Arden
for a sixty-dollar paraffin pedicure
that would begin to fill in the cracks.

Ich Bin Ein New Yorker

There would be no theater,
I was my own drama.
I and the shroud of Death
that said, no, we have not come to
fit you today.
Instead, fireworks played the midnight sky
over the Hudson and
Michael translated from
the Hebrew: life is not like a dick;
life is always hard.
You can't get this kind of healing
in the branch office.

New York, darling.
Your spirit fires mine even as it did that
decades-ago August when I arrived a refugee
from the—middle west.
Were you a man, my love,
you couldn't pry me out of bed.

Cut!

Sarah Jessica Parker.
Mary Louise Parker.
Mary Louise Wilson.
Mary Stuart Masterson.
Mary Elizabeth Mastrantonio.
    You people with your one-too-many names:
David Hyde Pierce,
David Ogden Stiers,
Haley Joel Osment,
    are knaves, knives that hack
    at the battered remains of my brain.
Robert Sean Leonard.
Seann William Scott.
Kristin Scott Thomas.
    Three is a crowd allowed
    for triptychs, triples and triplets,
    wishes, witches and crowns
    Strike three,
Jennifer Jason Leigh,
Jamie Lee Curtis,
Julia Louis-Dreyfus.
    Three cheers for musketeers, little kittens
    and visually-challenged mice.
Philip Baker Hall.
Philip Seymour Hoffman.
Billy Bob Thornton.
    Ménage a trois? Oui, we will need three,
    but I'm going to count to two now.
Ava Gardner.
Cary Grant.

Missing, Redux

Things, it seems, are not bad enough.
This morning on the crowded 151,
a little red-hoodie'd ingénue
looked up—at me—and said:
"Would you like to sit down?"
"Would you like to sit down?"

When, exactly, did I achieve the look
of a woman who is asked that?
True, I am on the sunset side of sexagenarianism.
And yes, the ophthalmologist is keeping an eye
on the ever-so-embryonic cataract.
And, what is that chronic twinge in my foot anyway?
But, *"Would you like to sit down?"*

Please. Do not ask that again.
Not 'til I've bought and paid for and am actually
wearing the flesh-colored, elastic stockings.

The Stories

Typing Lessons

Writing about Dan Rosen is embarrassing. There is naïve and there is NAÏVE.

I had just turned nineteen and needed a summer job after sophomore year at the University of Detroit. Working part-time at a local pharmaceutical company had run its course. A fledgling romance with a salesman had fizzled; I had an aching crush on the owner's brother, and the work itself was deadly—typing and filing doctors' names and addresses on translucent stencils and proofreading for the advertising manager. It was he who one day said: "You should be a copywriter." Not knowing what that was, I looked it up: one who writes copy.

"I'm looking for a summer job," I told the woman in a neighborhood loan office. "Can you type?" Yes, I said, tentatively, wondering if my two-fingered experience counted. "Let's see you copy this letter." She left the room, and I rolled a sheet of paper into the typewriter.

I could opt for accuracy and hunt and peck, but if the woman were listening, she'd hear that I was no typist. Or, I could let my fingers fly and sound like the real thing. It pains me to say that the hapless Polish streak in me won. The letter I handed to the woman was largely gibberish. I left the office jobless and humiliated.

"Doctor's Receptionist" called out the ad in the help wanted section. Perhaps there would be no typing; I'd simply wear white, smile sympathetically and usher not overly sick people into small rooms.

"Oh you're too qualified," said the misguided soul at the

agency, looking over my application. Maybe the job had already been filled or maybe the headline was just a come-on.

"How would you like to work for BBDO, the advertising agency?" Batten, Barton, Durstine & Osborn was Jack Benny's agency, and he used to joke about the name. I could work for people who worked for Jack Benny? "Okay!"

The receptionist on the eighteenth floor in the Penobscot Building was on the phone. "I have the world's worst stomach ache." I'd never heard "world's worst;" I was captivated.

Personnel manager, Mary Valentine, was the tall, iron-grey-haired antithesis of her merry, heart-shaped name. "You would be secretary to the two copywriters. You type, yes?" "Mmmm, yes." Telling the truth would have meant losing Jack Benny. I held my breath fearing the typing test. It never came.

"This isn't a summer job," Mary warned. "You're not going back to school in September, are you?" "No." Yes, I was going back, but I couldn't say that and kill my chance to work with people who got paid to put words on paper. A baby writer was ready to be born, and the humorless woman across the desk appeared to be the midwife.

Jim Denny was a white-faced, dark-haired, beefy and pro-fessionally friendly man who had lost a leg in World War II. A picture of his wife and four children, including a daughter named Feather, was propped on his desk amid piles of chaos.

Dan Rosen was six-four with a nose too small for his face and a crew cut that, at twenty-nine, was already more salt than pepper. A New Yorker, Dan had recently been hired to work on the DeSoto business.

"There can't be any erasures on this," he said the next morning handing me a yellow sheet of copy. "And I need one and eight." "One and eight?" "An original and eight carbons."

My typewriter was outside his office. I placed eight sheets of carbon paper between eight sheets of white paper. There would be no flying fingers this time, and I hoped that Dan had better things to do than listen.

Careful though I was, I had scarcely got past "Chrysler Corporation. DeSoto. 60 second Radio" when I typed a v for a b. No erasures, he said. Maybe he wouldn't notice just this one. I tore eight strips of paper and placed them between the carbons and copies to execute an invisible fix, but as I lifted the original, I saw the first carbon's inky side facing up; the words were copied backwards on the wrong side of the paper. A quick check showed all eight carbons facing the wrong way. Uh-oh.

Praying that Dan would stay put and spare me from being fired the day after I was hired, I yanked the aborted one-and-eight from the typewriter, placed them upside down in the wastebasket and prepared a new batch, carbons facing down this time.

"Chrysler Corporation. DeSoto. 60 second Radio. Bob Reynoldz." Oops! This time, I slipped the strips of paper between the properly aligned carbons and copies and erased the errant letter, but no; the smudge was obvious. Nothing to do but toss the whole business and start over. Not that that attempt would prove luckier than the previous two. In fact, there would be nearly two dozen one-and-eights tossed at first into the wastebasket then, fearing being caught wasting, into my purse, then the bin in the ladies' room, and, finally, carted home for disposal.

Dan, thankfully, was occupied with work and calls and seemingly unaware that it had taken me all day to type a few hundred, unerased words. I, however, was a sweating wreck of nerves and on my way home bought a typing manual.

After dinner, I set up shop on a nightstand in my room and studied the diagram that showed where to place each finger, managing in fairly quick order, to get the hang of it but allowing my right pinkie to remain unengaged as it remains to this day.

I was born to type; two days later, I was turning in impeccable pages, and in a week I was bored. "Can't I do something creative?" I asked Dan. He answered with a question some variation of which I would hear for the next thirty-five years: "You want to write a commercial?" "Okay."

Back to my home office on the nightstand. And back the next morning with a commercial that the men liked well enough to put on the air. Suddenly the copy department had three writers and, almost as suddenly, Dan was asking me to work late on Thursday nights.

The work, or rather the ruse, was over the minute everyone else in the office cleared out, and then we too were out and on our way to dinners at the Ponchartrain Wine Cellar, London Chop House or Sinbad's on the river.

Dan introduced me to the martinis that set my embryonic

Typing Lessons

alcoholic circuitry sizzling, lit our Kents, said I should know Dave Brubeck and Norman Mailer, spun heady stories of New York and the marvels on Lexington, including the new Manhattan House where we might actually live; and oh, his wife, Sandy, a nice enough girl, had a nameless life-threatening but not debilitating illness which somehow manifested itself in her not understanding him (so much for creativity), and how would it be if we drove over to Belle Isle and parked for a while so he could continue his ongoing lessons in what made for good advertising, the tutorial interrupted by a goodly amount of groping.

One day, Dan said Sandy would be away visiting family so we should have dinner at his place, and he'd cook his famous steak burgers with melted Roquefort inside. And so he did, but not before we shared a pitcher of gin and vermouth, and not before I was under him on the sofa, and he was clamping his hand over my mouth so the neighbors wouldn't hear the scream that signaled the demise of my maidenhood; and then we had the burgers.

Driving myself home that night, I worried that people would look at me and know. I should have been worried about the pain I had just taken on. Oh, please let Sandy hurry up and die so Dan and I can marry and live glamorously ever after, oh please.

But now the only mention of plans for us dealt with which hotel and when. I lived for our lunches and Thursday nights and dreaded the empty weekends. Meanwhile, another secretary, herself a New York transplant, said, "Detroit's a car town; if you want to get ahead, you need to go to New York."

Typing Lessons

That's the ticket. Get out from under this miserable affair and have a career. I shared the latter idea with Dan who spoke with the head of the agency who wrote a letter introducing me to the New York office. Lovely, but I wanted to do this myself. Of the fifty agencies I wrote to looking for a job as copywriter, twelve wrote back saying, forget it; another twelve said, come ahead.

But what if I get a job and then can't write? Jim Denny said, "Don't worry about it. Good, bad or indifferent, the words will come."

Mom said, "You'll be back; you'll never hear the alarm." Daddy said, "You can come home anytime."

On a sunny morning in August, friends drove me to the airport, and I cried my way to LaGuardia.

Dan's sister, a model for Pauline Trigére, lived at Mrs. Ferguson's residence for women on Madison and 68th Street. She arranged for me to move into a corner room and, from one of its windows, I could see Central Park.

Somewhere, trumpets were blaring: welcome home, little bumpkin. On the first afternoon of my shiny new life, I opened a checking account at Chase Manhattan (I liked the name), bought a periwinkle cashmere sweater (the start of a long sub-career in drunken sailor spending), and went to the top of the Empire State Building where a man asked me to have dinner; I was too shy to accept.

The next day, I made my twelve calls.

Mom was half right. I slept through a morning appointment at Y&R; the next two places wanted a secretary who could spell. Day three, I called BBDO for an interview.

Wearing a camel cotton dress with white piping, and, having taken off the white gloves, I waved around my letter from the boondocks and was hired as a copywriter. $85 a week. This called for shopping.

I opened a charge at Lord and Taylor and bought a pair of $28 Ferragamos. I would have bought an Hermes bag, not yet named Kelly, as well, except it was $300. (Ah, for the grace of foresight. Today's leather Kelly is $4700; the crocodile, $17,000).

Dan came to New York on business. Monkey business, too, for a while. Thinking I was pregnant at one point, I called him in a panic. I expected: There, there, Darling; not to worry. What I got was chilly annoyance—just this side of: Do I know you?

And that's when I woke up.

Ten years later, I learned that Dan had divorced, remarried, fathered a child, and died of cirrhosis of the liver. He was forty-four.

Remembering Jody Silver

I'm not sure which came first, Marjorie Morningstar or Jody Silver, the copywriter I shared a grey cubicle with on Madison Avenue in the late fifties. Both were Central Park West Jewish, privileged, gorgeous, cocky and irresistible. Jody and her brand of whip-smart sass lit into my life and set it spinning.

I have always been star struck. At five, in the sunny kitchen of my uncle's rectory in Coraopolis, Pennsylvania, I talked to a girl who said she was ten. Ten? The thought of achieving that heady number, so beyond the mere one digits, was my first step on a relentless course of upward.

In fourth grade, it was pale, silent Dawn Okie who I examined for clues as to why her projects were so exquisite, so flawless, while mine were so humanly unremarkable. Had I directed that energy toward arithmetic, my checkbook today might be not be littered with arrows and question marks.

Later, all-girls Dominican High raneth over with no end of intriguers: elegant Gabrielle Padelt, cashmere'd Joan Resseguie, and a purportedly Mafia-connected girl who one day showed up with a three-carat diamond engagement ring. In pre-Elizabethan Taylor days, three looked like thirty-three.

Freshman year at college, it was the silky, milky, homecoming-queenly Beverly White. Not content to swing her champagne pageboy in my face, Beverly managed to nab the skittish Flanagan, man of my then and entirely too many future dreams who had told a mutual friend I was too sophisticated for him. a) I didn't know what sophisticated meant. b) I wouldn't be it anymore. c) It didn't matter.

Remembering Jody Silver

Shortly after I launched my New York life, Jody Silver was delivered to my lab like a rare orchid, and my microscope was quivering.

I was in the group headed by the hat-wearing-in-the-office Margery Fowler who sang out the word *Wonderful!* in a way that made you believe it. Our job was to write commercials for Campbell Soup, Wisk and FTD. My line for the latter: "Flowers—the shortest distance between two hearts" was the first in a series of campaigns that, for one or another disheartening reason, would abort within the Agency.

Jody's assignment was to write a radio commercial for that week's edition of The Saturday Evening Post. Period. No sitting in tedious meetings; no reporting to higher ups. Jody had a singular arrangement, thanks to the Agency president, whom she referred to as Bills.

I dutifully arrived at the office at nine and started flailing. At 9:15, the mail boy delivered two red roses to Jody's desk, compliments of Elliot Farnsworth, an antiques dealer of the Clifton Webb variety and one of her regular dinner companions. Elliot sent them every other morning and might still except that I just read his obituary in The Times.

On the dot of 9:45, or close enough, Jody—all naturally curly (naturally), ebony-eyed, five feet of her—blew in wearing one of her numerous little tailored suits and linen blouses, shot me a quick Hi Lulu, and promptly got to work on the stack of pink phone messages that had piled up in her absence.

Writing that lone radio spot took Jody a single afternoon.

Remembering Jody Silver

The result was a snappy pastiche of questions designed to lure the unwary listener, the articles never as seductive as Jody's bait. The remaining hours, aside from the two at lunch when she had her hair done or a manicure or massage, were spent writing her first play, sharing thoughts about clothes and jewelry, theater and men, restaurants and travel, and, occasionally practicing her camped up rendition of "Witchcraft."

The actual lunch part of Jody's lunch was chicken salad on toast, the crusts of which she would remove and arrange as she chatted on the phone, gold bracelets clinking.

"Come for a drink tonight," she said one afternoon. So, after work, we took a taxi to 79th Street where Jody and the roommate she called The Duchess, but who, in fact, was the daughter of a Rhinebeck realtor, lived in a spacious two-bedroom flat. I sat on the brocade sofa and studied the props of someone who didn't live paycheck-to-paycheck: serious furniture, heavy lamps, good rugs on polished wood.

Jody brought a tray with crystal glasses of scotch, Finn crisps, a pepper shaker and mound of ground sirloin. "Here, I poured us a hooker," she said handing me a glass then spreading the crackers with her version of steak tartare.

We gossiped a while then, looking at her watch, she said, "Oh, I've got to pop into a tub. Stay and talk to me? We'll just leave these things for the maid."

The closet in Jody's bedroom with burgundy velvet spread and paintings in gilt frames was crammed with silk and satin dresses; high heels spilled from Bergdorf boxes. I stood, hooker in hand, while she pulled out a deep green Scaasi ("That's Isaacs backwards, Lulu.").

"Come with us. Harold Goldflies is taking me to the Little Club." "Oh, but I'm not dressed." "Don't be silly. You look fine." Wearing a nothing skirt and sweater, I looked secretarial at best, but arguing was fruitless, and, besides, I was curious.

Jody was out for dinner six nights a week with six different escorts; Sunday was family night on Central Park West. Where they came from, her unending stream of, for the most part, much older men with apparently unending cash, I couldn't imagine.

There was a whole other New York of style and substance; penthouses, country houses and servants; confidence and clubs; dressmakers and dividends; huge talent and easy laughter; all of it beyond my reach. Darn it. Next time, my parents would be old money. All I could do for the moment was take notes.

Harold came by at eight, and we headed to the bôite where we joined the merrymakers whose perfect lives were rendered even more perfect at the sight of at least two of us. "Jodeee!" "Darling!" "You look divine!" "Harold, you old bastard!" "We were wondering if you'd show. We need someone to pick up the check!"

There were drinks and more drinks; nothing resembling a move to order food, and I was storing data on how the very other half plays. The ravishing focus was ever Jody, firing off the inspired retort, leaning over for a light, throwing her head back at yet another hilarious morsel.

Finally, the hour arrived when it wasn't inappropriate to eat, and we each were obliterated by a mammoth white menu with sobering prices. Everyone ordered steak. Jody dined in slow motion, cutting away the unacceptable outer rim of her filet, moving pieces of the next segment in some arcane ritual, then nibbling the merest bites of the bleeding center.

Occasionally thereafter, I (chronically dateless and dressed closer to the fives than the nines but apparently amusing enough to be included) joined Jody & Company at San Marino, Mercurio, Danny's Hideaway or Orsini's where Armando in white dinner jacket offered insider information on the fare. Always arugula. The very name thrilled me. Where had this zippy stuff been all my pale life?

Jody's striking mother, Wall Street father, and Ruth Gordony grandmother lived in a Hannah & Her Sisters apartment filled with well-worn rugs and art that said have a drink and worry about nothing. Granny held court in a curtained bed strewn with jewelry and scarves, biscuits and tea. Visitors were expected to pull up a chair and provide an audience for the dowager. "She's outrageous, Lulu; she mixes costume pieces with the real stuff." And you thought Coco Chanel invented that.

People are like courses. Some we take for a few months, some for decades. Jody and I lost touch after two years. Rather, I spun off the curriculum. What was a little girl from Wilmerding, PA doing in an honors class in Posh?

My path led me to marriage, motherhood, lingering post-partum blues, and a continuing career in Chicago; Jody's (documented in the columns) took her to marriage to a celebrated plastic surgeon, palaces on Fifth Avenue, in the Hamptons and Palm Springs and pals like Bernstein and Billy Rose, Sinatra and Jule Styne.

Years later, out from under my depression and sturdy enough, well sort of, for Jody and the jet lane, I sent her a warm, funny note hoping to reconnect. Perhaps lunch on my next visit to New York?

Ms. Silver's secretary phoned with regrets.

"Can't You Two Just Have A Long Affair?"

It was her desperation speaking. Poor Bertie. How could her son, the handsome Jewish prince, want to marry the impoverished shiksa from someplace called Detroit?

Not that she disliked me; it was the lack of important family and riches (of even the nouveau variety) to back me up; and a million years ago, in the fifties, intermarriage was no small matter either.

To silence our respective Greek choruses—my own family was no less anti the union; they liked Marty, but, my God, he was Jewish—we burrowed ever deeper into each other's arms and married. They were right to object but not for those reasons. One of the upsides of our psychic mis-match, aside from two delicious daughters, was that I got to study Bertie.

On summer Friday nights in pre-children New York, we left our two-bedroom, $200 rent-controlled apartment on 90th and Park for Bertie and Jack's white-pillared, Georgian mansion in Long Beach, Long Island. A reflection of her passion for all things Williamsburg, the house was built for them in 1920 for $60,000.

The right wing was designated by a white-lettered, black iron sign: J. J. Blinn, M.D.. Inside were a waiting room and small office for Jack and his nurse, Dorothy Ross, who bristled with purpose and who Bertie, envious of Jack's respect for his assistant, referred to as Poughkeepsie Rose. (She wasn't from Poughkeepsie; Bertie used the phrase to suggest hayseed.)

The examining room included a refrigerator with, among medical accoutrement, boxes of dark chocolates. If you were a Blinn, you disdained the milk variety, and the candy had to be

"Can't You Two Just Have A Long Affair?"

cold. The laboratory in the basement conjured Dr. Hyde.

The front door of the house opened to a foyer with a tall staircase, grandmother clock and Queen Anne settee upholstered in yellow silk damask seen only when its ivory cotton slipcover was out for cleaning. "This is so beautiful," I said admiring the shimmery fabric and wishing Bertie would connect my words with a willingness to forgo the covering, but no. If she didn't agree, she didn't answer suggesting that your idea was so appalling, it didn't merit comment.

Inspired by a gorgeous terrace Marty and I had recently seen on Capri, I plunged right in with, "How about red geraniums and white petunias, for a change?" Bertie, whose own terrace was ringed each year with a splendid mix of salmon geraniums and periwinkle ageratum, responded with silence. No doubt she was being, what she called, diplomatic; Bertie was keen on diplomacy, frequently citing the lack of it in whomever.

The Wedgwood blue living room, thirty-five feet long with fifteen-foot ceilings, held a matching blue silk sofa flanked by tables with silvered lamps, a grand piano played by no one, a huge red Oriental rug, a pair of crimson silk wing back chairs, a curlicue-legged rocker in chartreuse chinoiserie, small tables with antiques and, above the fireplace, an oil portrait of the royalty themselves, Marty aged ten and brother Bruce, eight. The room was an empty stage; there was no entertaining. Bertie was too depressed and hypercritical to cultivate friendships, and such family as there was she found wanting.

As a child, she was a clever, dimpled darling whose father, a

"Can't You Two Just Have A Long Affair?"

successful clothier, lavished her with a princess's wardrobe, approval, and affection. In her twenties, she fell in love with a fantasy with beautiful hands, mistook his quiet manner for sensitivity and was forever after the disappointed bride.

Whatever creative energy Bertie might have parlayed into a career in antiques (she had a keen eye and was a helluva gabber) was impounded by her unhappiness. Leaving Jack would have required more emotional grit than she could summon, and therapy wasn't an option; she had written off the entire medical profession as arrogant menaces who would side with her husband.

Bertie's days, after breakfast in the Tiffany-shaded octagonal breakfast room, began with meal planning with Nora, the dour cook. "Whatever you do, don't ask how she is," Bertie warned. "She'll say, 'About the same.'" I'd forget and ask then wince as the morose little soul answered on cue.

A no-nonsense shopper, Bertie made frequent trips in her immaculate white Buick convertible (chamois'd every day by the handyman as was Jack's forest green Cadillac) to her favorite market, Waldbaums. The woman knew her honeydew and standing rib roast.

Her rare appearances in the cavernous industrial-white kitchen produced a limited repertoire: a superb chicken soup (kosher chicken, fresh dill), purportedly celestial sweet-and-sour calves' tongues that never touched mine, and a sublime chopped liver; the last accompanied by Saturday night cocktails, well, cocktail. Jack frowned on more than the singular: "That stuff's intoxicating." Right again.

"Can't You Two Just Have A Long Affair?"

Bertie also knew her Loehmann's. ("Originally $250, marked down to $100, I got it for $30"). But where she truly shone was in her ability to unearth the finest treasures for the tiniest price from the dustiest thrift shop. Dusty was key; if a place was "too cleaned up," it would yield no bargain.

In the years I knew her, Bertie was a beauty shop blonde who wrapped her sturdy curls in a faded chiffon scarf, puffed but didn't inhale Pall Malls as she rubbed Brasso over her latest acquisition, and droned a melancholy monologue of variations on a theme of Jack and his shortcomings.

Her deadpan delivery of quirky put-downs—"He's as cold as a dead sturgeon."—struck me as funny, and I often laughed inappropriately. Years later, seeing a photograph of our fifteen-year old Meredith's first beau, she encouraged us to "close on the deal." And she liked trying on alternatives to her loathed given name, Bertha; the more affected, the better. "What do you think of Bettina? Belinda? Babette?"

Bertie's stream-of-conscious Jackonian diatribe was occasionally interrupted with a directive to me: "You should write a book." It was a message within a message: You can create something other than advertising, and you're looking at rich material.

Afternoons, after excursions for food or treasure, Bertie nestled into the long gold sofa in the apple green sunroom and rested. Nobody in my family rested. We didn't have allergies either. These exotica belonged to another culture. Bertie looked so cozy under her yellow knitted afghan, I memorized

"Can't You Two Just Have A Long Affair?"

her for the someday I might slow down enough to rest.

In the evenings, Jack sat in the easy chair opposite the sofa; and in a corner across the room, a TV occupied a shallow, green-tiled pool that had been stocked with goldfish when the boys were small.

Three blocks from the powdery board-walked beach and close to Reynolds Channel for Saturday morning fluke fishing, the house was an almost-free bed & breakfast & lunch & dinner. The tariff was having to witness the bleak dynamics of a marriage that hung together on ill-fitting hinges. Theirs, not ours.

"Easy on the bread, Bert," Jack would admonish at Edoard's steak house, thereby effectively raining on one of his wife's few parades. A silent, icy martinet who in his youth taught himself not to laugh because it aggravated his asthma, he was your basic warm, caring, house-calling doctor, i.e., God; and he was held in high regard by his colleagues.

A lifelong student, Jack added cardiology to his practice of internal medicine, pored over his Spanish textbooks (Marty doubted he could put a whole sentence together), and founded the Long Beach public library.

My upbeat demeanor was anathema to Jack's chilly reserve. Oh, for a daughter-in-law, the physicist, rather than a Madison Avenue madcap. There were no outbreaks, both of us being controlled and disliking scenes, but he made me feel insubstantial as a butterfly.

Despite the nightly therapeutic Dubonnet he sipped with a grimace, Jack, at seventy-three, was felled by a heart attack

"Can't You Two Just Have A Long Affair?"

and left his widow without the object of her misery. Might she be free, finally, to realize an even minimally happier life? No. Bertie cleared out of the house (per their plan, it was given to the hospital and became a nurses' dorm) and moved to the city where she holed up in the old Alrae Hotel and hired a joyless companion to fix simple meals and provide an ear for the past tense version of Jack stories.

Marty and I had relocated to Chicago by then, and I'd visit her when I came to New York to shoot commercials.

"I know you're busy, Lucia, but when I die, I want you to take a week and go through all my things. Will you do that?"

"Absolutely."

Without Jack for distraction, her depression took over, and Bertie gave up. Poking around the city's thrift shops held no appeal; and she couldn't mobilize herself to come see us in "your Chicago," a place that she—a New Yorker of the Steinberg/Hudson River type—found corny and quaint yet somehow endearing.

As one who had escaped the Midwest, embraced Manhattan as home and, thanks to Marty's work, was dragged back, whining, to the hinterland, I was infuriated by her condescension.

Bertie took to her bed, prayed to die, and her faulty heart obliged within a year.

"It's not going to happen that way," some wag said about making plans. A few days before Bertie's death, our housekeeper slipped on a patch of ice and broke both arms. So much

"Can't You Two Just Have A Long Affair?"

for taking a week to go through her things.

Having no one to stay with our daughters, I flew to New York for the service, quickly chose some jewelry and silver, arranged shipping for a Victorian chair and bombé chest, and flew home leaving Marty and Bruce to deal with closing the apartment.

Marty called the following day. "We found a key to a locked closet."

"*What?? What's in it?*" Oh God. This is what she meant about going through her things. Why hadn't she told me about or even shown me the closet?

"Oh, a lot of stuff, big stuff. That giant silver venison thing." A faint memory, years before, Bertie saying, "This belonged to Marion Davies."

"Trust me, we don't have room for any of it. We're calling an auction house."

Why didn't I fly in for a day? Why didn't I leave the girls with a friend? What was I thinking? Or drinking?

They're out there somewhere—Bertie's things, my things, her granddaughters' things. Perhaps the venison server gleams on a sideboard in Scarsdale; a tole tray may have wound up in Chelsea; a Chinese rug on Staten Island. Or, possibly, they've come full circle, and a handsome sterling jug awaits its next owner in a tony shop on Madison, or, needing a good polishing, goes unnoticed in a properly dusty Brooklyn thrift shop.

They're just things and, these alarming days, scarcely an issue. Still, the words, "...a key to a locked closet" have yet to lose their sting.

The Author

Lucia Blinn is a poet, writer and storyteller.
She has performed her work at the Chicago Humanities
Festival, National Foundation for Jewish Culture's
Literary Salon, Heartland Spa and Recorded Art Works.
The stories in this volume are excerpted from her
memoir-in-progress.

A former advertising creative director,
Lucia is the mother of two far-flung daughters and is
a gardener who tends two balconies high above
Lincoln Park in Chicago.

Bouquets of Thanks

To publisher, Lorelei Bendinger, the all-knowing,
all-conjuring siren I might not know were it not for
Nina (Life is a Party) Baker Feinberg;

Bruce Bendinger, the smart writer I knew in the ad old
days who grew up even smarter;

art director, Alvin Blick, who has never had a small idea;

photographer, Steve Ewert, who thought we were
shooting a postage stamp, not wallpaper;

Mary Hutchings Reed for the lawyering;

my darling Meredith for the re-re-revisions;

Dick McKee and Malloy for the impeccable printing;
my coterie of cheerers-on;

and The Daffodil for the last word(s).

Did I say bouquets? Make it acres of orchids.